GW00320300

Never Too Old

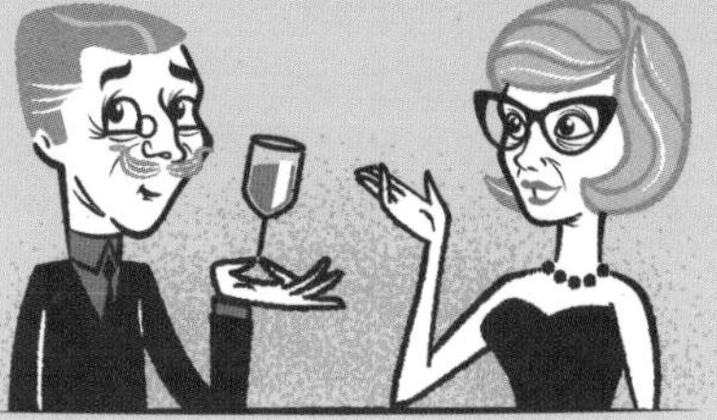

for all your gift books and gift stationery

Published in 2017 by Allsorted.
Watford, Hertfordshire,
WD19 4BG
U.K.

© Susanna Geoghegan Gift Publishing 2017
Concept by Milestone Design
Compiled by Michael Powell & Fiona Thornton
Designed by Joanna Ross at Double Fish Design Ltd
Illustrated by Dave Williams

ISBN: 978-1-910562-96-3

Printed in China

Every effort has been made to ensure the accuracy of the
information contained in this book.
In the unlikely case of queries please contact the compilers
via their website www.susannageoghegan.com.

Never Too Old

You are never too old to set another goal or to dream another dream, perform your first parachute jump, have a novel published, take up marathon running, climb the world's highest mountains, travel to the North Pole, take up pole dancing, fly into space, graduate from college, get a tattoo, ride the biggest rollercoasters, become a famous painter or competitive water skier, take up bodybuilding or bungee jump.

The reason we can say this with absolute confidence is that this book is filled with dozens of real-life stories of older people doing these remarkable things – in their sixties, seventies, eighties, nineties and even as centenarians.

It also spotlights the happiness and longevity secrets of some of the longest-lived people on the planet. Despite their impressive feats, they are mostly ordinary people who decided to follow their passions and who refused to allow their numerical age to be an obstacle.

There are also lots of sassy and humorous quotations about growing old to remind you that you're never alone in facing the challenges and absurdities of the third age.

Surprise Surprise

ON 19TH MARCH, 2011 FORREST LUNSWAY AND ROSE POLLARD BECAME THE WORLD'S OLDEST NEWLYWEDS WHEN THEY MARRIED IN CALIFORNIA ON THE GROOM'S 100TH BIRTHDAY. THE BRIDE WAS 93.

The stunned wedding guests believed that they were attending a birthday party, but they were delighted to discover that the two lovebirds, with a combined age of 193, had decided to make their union official after dating for 28 years.

They first met at a seniors' ballroom dance. Their advice for a happy relationship is: 'Be forgiving and patient and say "I love you" once in a while.' Forrest's secret to longevity is the odd glass of wine and a life spent outdoors rather than in an office. His favourite food is '… fried food. Something you can get a chunk of. Cut a bite off a piece of meat, that's what I like.' He also long ago quit his 27-year habit of smoking a packet of cigarettes every day.

Initially, Rose had no desire to get married, but agreed after Forrest asked, 'How come we never got married?' Her reply was, 'Because you never asked me.' So he proposed and she agreed to marry him on his hundredth birthday.

After the wedding, Forrest promised: 'We've got many happy years left as I intend to stick around until I'm at least 110. You've got to use it or lose it.'

One good thing about getting older is that if you're getting married, the phrase 'till death do you part' doesn't sound so horrible. It only means about 10 or 15 years and not the eternity it used to mean.

Joy Behar

A woman has the age she deserves.

Coco Chanel

ONE OF THE GREATEST PLEASURES OF GROWING OLD IS LOOKING BACK AT THE PEOPLE YOU DIDN'T MARRY.

Elizabeth Taylor

A CENTENARIAN IS A PERSON WHO HAS LIVED TO BE 100 YEARS OF AGE. HE NEVER SMOKED OR HE SMOKED ALL HIS LIFE. HE NEVER DRANK WHISKEY OR HE DRANK WHISKEY FOR 80 YEARS. HE WAS A VEGETARIAN OR HE WASN'T A VEGETARIAN. FOLLOW THESE RULES CLOSELY AND YOU TOO CAN BECOME A CENTENARIAN.

Stephen Leacock

You end up as you deserve. In old age you must put up with the face, the friends, the health, and the children you have earned.

Fay Weldon

Happiness is good health and a bad memory.

Ingrid Bergman

THE OLDER I GROW, THE MORE I LISTEN TO PEOPLE WHO DON'T SAY MUCH.

Germain G. Glidden

PERHAPS ONE HAS TO BE VERY OLD BEFORE ONE LEARNS TO BE AMUSED RATHER THAN SHOCKED.

Pearl S. Buck

Vera Lynn: National Treasure

ON D-DAY WEEKEND IN 2014, 97-YEAR-OLD DAME VERA LYNN MADE BRITISH CHART HISTORY BY BECOMING THE OLDEST LIVING ARTIST TO REACH THE TOP 20 OF THE UK'S OFFICIAL ALBUMS CHART.

The Forces' Sweetheart entered the UK's Official Albums Chart at Number 13 with her new collection, Vera Lynn: National Treasure. The double album, released by Decca Records to mark the 70th anniversary of the D-Day landings, featured such seminal songs as 'We'll Meet Again' and '(There'll Be Bluebirds Over) The White Cliffs Of Dover' as well as three recently discovered tracks.

Five years earlier she had become the oldest living artist to reach Number 1 in the UK's Official Albums Chart with We'll Meet Again: The Very Best of Vera Lynn, a selection of her recordings from between 1936 and 1959. A staggering 57 years before that she had become the first foreign artist to top the Billboard Chart in the US with 'Auf Wiedersehen Sweetheart' (where it remained for nine weeks) in 1952.

'I am delighted!' Dame Vera Lynn told the Official Charts Company. 'It is wonderful to hear these songs again, and it's warming to think that everyone else is listening to them, too.'

> IT'S TRUE, SOME WINES IMPROVE WITH AGE. BUT ONLY IF THE GRAPES WERE GOOD IN THE FIRST PLACE.
>
> *Abigail Van Buren*

No Limits

YOGA MASTER TAO PORCHON-LYNCH HAD JUST TURNED 87 WHEN SHE BROKE HER HIP AFTER FALLING OUTSIDE A GROCERY STORE. AFTER THE RESULTING OPERATION, HER DOCTOR INFORMED HER STERNLY THAT IT WAS TIME TO SLOW DOWN AND ACCEPT THE LIMITATIONS OF HER AGEING BODY.

One month after surgery, she took up ballroom dancing. Five years later in 2012, she and her 23-year-old dance partner were touring the world taking part in ballroom dancing competitions. She was also teaching at least 12 yoga classes a week.

Tao sent a photo of herself to the same doctor. It showed the 93-year-old outside the Taj Mahal, supporting her entire weight on her hands whilst sitting in the Lotus Position. The caption read: 'I just wanted to show you that there's nothing you can't do.' The doctor was so impressed and humbled that the photo is proudly displayed in his office.

The same year, she entered the Guinness Book of World Records as the world's oldest yoga instructor. When she was 98 years old she published her autobiography, Dancing Light: The Spiritual Side of Being Through the Eyes of a Modern Yoga Master, which won an Independent Publisher Book Award and International Book Awards in three categories.

Let's Get Physical

Bob, an 82-year-old man, went to the doctor for a check-up. A few days later, the doctor saw him walking down the street with a gorgeous young woman on his arm. At his follow-up appointment she said to Bob, 'You're really doing great, aren't you?'

Bob replied, 'I'm just doing what you said, Doc: "Get a hot mamma and be cheerful".'

'I didn't say that,' replied the doctor. 'I said, "You've got a heart murmur, be careful".'

THE SECRET OF LONGEVITY IS TO KEEP

BREATHING.

Sophie Tucker

I DON'T EXERCISE. IF GOD WANTED ME TO BEND OVER, HE'D HAVE PUT DIAMONDS ON THE FLOOR.

Joan Rivers

AFTER 40 A WOMAN HAS TO CHOOSE BETWEEN LOSING HER FIGURE OR HER FACE. MY ADVICE IS TO KEEP YOUR FACE, AND STAY SITTING DOWN.

Barbara Cartland

With sixty staring me in the face, I have developed inflammation of the sentence structure and a definite hardening of the paragraphs.

James Thurber

TIME MAY BE A GREAT HEALER, BUT IT'S A TERRIBLE BEAUTICIAN.

OH, I WAS SO MUCH OLDER THEN;
I'M YOUNGER THAN THAT

NOW.

Bob Dylan

I ADVISE YOU TO GO ON LIVING SOLELY TO ENRAGE THOSE
WHO ARE PAYING YOUR ANNUITIES. IT IS THE ONLY
PLEASURE I HAVE LEFT.

Voltaire

The Invisible Wall

HARRY BERNSTEIN WAS 24 WHEN HE HAD A SHORT STORY ACCEPTED FOR PUBLICATION IN A MAGAZINE IN 1934. BUT HE HAD TO WAIT ANOTHER 72 YEARS TO FIND LITERARY SUCCESS WITH HIS BESTSELLING MEMOIR.

He had lived almost an entire lifetime between these two publishing milestones. The Invisible Wall, published by Random House in 2007, describes his poverty-stricken childhood in a Cheshire mill town, his abusive alcoholic father and the anti-Semitism his family and neighbours experienced, as well as a star-crossed romance involving his eldest sister and her Christian boyfriend.

Harry had spent much of his life in publishing, reading books and scripts for a film studio and editing a trade magazine for builders, and he even had a novel published in 1981, but fame and fortune eluded him.

The impetus for writing his memoir was the death from leukaemia of Ruby, his beloved wife of 67 years. Consumed with loneliness and grief, Harry sought solace in his childhood memories to see him through the long sleepless nights. It was a revelation: 'I realised then why I had failed in writing novels, because I turned away from personal experience and depended on imagination.' But he also recognised that his time had come: 'If I had not lived until I was 90, I would not have been able to write this book.'

> OLD WOOD BEST TO BURN, OLD WINE TO DRINK, OLD FRIENDS TO TRUST, AND OLD AUTHORS TO READ.
> *Francis Bacon*

Sleeps Like A Teenager

FOR THE LAST SIX YEARS OF HER LIFE, SUPERCENTENARIAN KAMATO HONGO BECAME FAMOUS ON THE SOUTHERN JAPANESE ISLAND OF KYUSHU, FOR HER UNUSUAL HABIT OF SLEEPING FOR 48 HOURS AND THEN STAYING AWAKE FOR TWO DAYS.

Her sleeping patterns changed after she underwent hip surgery at the age of 110. Her family was concerned at first, then they decided to let her sleep when she wanted to, and not to try to wake her up. So she slept through her 114th birthday and she was also asleep when a certificate arrived in September 2002 confirming her inclusion in the Guinness Book of World Records as the oldest person in the world.

Family members would feed her small meals while she was asleep and her great-granddaughter, Tomoko Kurauchi, 18, reapplied her bright pink nail polish every day. She ate a healthy diet of fish, rice, pork, green tea and rice wine, with the occasional lump of unrefined brown sugar. She also had a positive outlook, which she believed was instrumental in her longevity. She took regular moderate exercise by performing elaborate traditional Japanese dance movements with her hands while confined to her bed. When she died on 31st October, 2003, she was 116 years and 45 days old.

Silver Surfer

An 80-year-old silver surfer was staying with his grown-up daughter. While he was visiting, he asked her for the password to the Wi-Fi.

'It's taped under the modem,' she told him.

After three failed attempts to log on, he asked, 'Am I spelling this right? T-A-P-E-D-U-N-D-E-R-T-H-E-M-O-D-E-M?'

EVERY WOMAN OVER FIFTY SHOULD STAY IN BED UNTIL NOON.

Mamie Eisenhower

NO DAY IS SO BAD IT CAN'T BE FIXED WITH A NAP.

Carrie Snow

IF WE SPENT AS MUCH TIME FEELING POSITIVE ABOUT GETTING OLDER, AS WE DO TRYING TO STAY YOUNG, HOW MUCH DIFFERENT OUR LIVES WOULD BE.

Rob Brown

Awkward Subject

A solicitor drafted wills for an elderly couple who were apprehensive about discussing death. When they arrived to sign the documents, she ushered them into her office, smiling broadly to put them at their ease.

'Now,' she said to them, 'which one of you wants to go first?'

I USUALLY TAKE A TWO-HOUR NAP FROM ONE TO FOUR.

Yogi Berra

I HAVE THE HEART OF A SMALL CHILD. I KEEP IT IN A JAR ON MY DESK.

Stephen King

A POSITIVE ATTITUDE MAY NOT SOLVE ALL YOUR PROBLEMS, BUT IT WILL ANNOY ENOUGH PEOPLE TO MAKE IT WORTH THE EFFORT.

Herm Albright

Jumping For Joy

ON 20TH NOVEMBER, 2011, PAT MOOREHEAD FROM CALIFORNIA SET THE WORLD RECORD FOR THE MOST SKYDIVES BY AN 80-YEAR-OLD. HE PERFORMED A STAGGERING 80 SKYDIVES IN ONE DAY TO CELEBRATE HIS BIRTHDAY.

The event took place at Skydive Elsinore, the longest-running skydiving operation in North America where Pat made his first jump in 1969. A seasoned skydiver with more than 6,100 jumps, Pat made 14 practice jumps the day before the big event to ensure everything went smoothly for his record attempt. Each jump took about five minutes. As soon as he landed he was given another parachute and sent back up in a tiny plane to 2,200 feet for the next dive. He completed his 80 jumps in less than 7 hours.

His feat helped raise funds for the construction of a National Skydiving Museum in Fredericksburg, Virginia, which promotes public education and awareness of the sport of skydiving.

Pat's 68-year-old wife Alicia shares his passion for skydiving. At the time she had performed over 2,700 jumps, since her first in 1978, and she holds several formation skydiving records. When they jump together, they always kiss just before exiting the plane (out of affection, she claims, not superstition).

Grandmother of Performance Art

MARINA ABRAMOVIĆ IS A YUGOSLAV-BORN ARTIST BASED IN NEW YORK, FAMOUS FOR MORE THAN 40 YEARS OF VISCERAL AND CHALLENGING PERFORMANCE ART THAT EXPLORES THE LIMITS OF THE HUMAN PSYCHE.

In 1974 her famous piece Rhythm 0 offered audience members a choice of 72 objects, from a feather boa to a loaded pistol, which they could use to inflict either pleasure or pain on her. The resulting sadism left her badly injured.

One of her more recent challenges – The Artist Is Present – took place at New York's Museum of Modern Art (MoMA) between March and May 2010 when she was 64. She sat immobile while spectators took turns to sit opposite her, while she maintained eye contact with them. She sat for a total of 736 hours and 30 minutes and faced 1,545 sitters. By the end of the performance, people were queuing through the night to sit with her. She was also visited by several celebrities including Lady Gaga, James Franco, Lou Reed and Bjork.

Her ex-lover and creative partner Ulay surprised her by appearing on the opening night, when she held his hand and broke down in tears. The video footage of the meeting has been viewed by millions on YouTube. Twenty-two years earlier they had famously ended their relationship by walking from opposite ends of the Great Wall of China to meet in the middle and say goodbye.

DANCE AS IF NO ONE IS WATCHING, SING AS IF NO ONE IS LISTENING AND LIVE EVERY DAY AS IF IT IS YOUR LAST.

I rather regret I haven't taken more drugs. Is it too late, at seventy, to try cocaine? Would it be dangerous or interesting?

Joan Bakewell

EVENTUALLY YOU WILL GET TO A POINT WHERE YOU STOP LYING ABOUT YOUR AGE AND START BRAGGING ABOUT IT.

TO BE YOUNG, REALLY YOUNG, TAKES A VERY

LONG TIME.

Pablo Picasso

MY FATHER KEPT SEVERAL PAIRS OF FALSE TEETH, ONE SET IN A JAR MARKED 'BEST PAIR', ANOTHER MARKED 'NEXT BEST' AND A THIRD MARKED 'NOT BAD'.

David Hockney

Favourable Odds

At his 103rd birthday party, Bernard was asked
if he thought that he'd be around for his 104th.
'I certainly do,' he replied. 'Statistics show that
very few people die between the ages
of 103 and 104.'

I WORK EVERY DAY AND I WANT TO DIE SHOUTING 'MIERDA'.

Joan Miró

MY WIFE AND I TOOK OUT
LIFE INSURANCE POLICIES ON
ONE ANOTHER, SO NOW IT'S
JUST A WAITING GAME.

Bill Dwyer

IF YOU LIVE TO BE 90 IN ENGLAND
AND CAN STILL EAT A BOILED EGG,
THEY THINK YOU DESERVE THE
NOBEL PRIZE.

Alan Bennett

Poker Face

BRUCE ATKINSON IS ONE OF BRITAIN'S TOP POKER PLAYERS; HE'S SHARP, CONFIDENT, ARTICULATE, IN HIS MID-SEVENTIES, PRESIDENT OF THE EUROPEAN POKER PLAYERS HALL OF FAME AND HE'S ALSO A PROFESSIONAL ELVIS IMPERSONATOR WHO HAS PERFORMED IN LAS VEGAS.

Born in 1940 in Brighton, Bruce has been playing poker for 35 years and describes himself as 'semi-professional'. He started to play Seven-Card Stud Hi-Lo in the UK during the seventies, then in the eighties he switched to Hold'em in Vegas. He earned his first winnings at the World Series of Poker in 1998, aged 58. His total live tournament winnings exceed $500,000.

His many years of experience show that he's in for the long haul, even though he has watched hi-rolling online poker players burst onto the World Series. Some of them win big but many lose their stacks quickly. 'You have to remember that if one person is winning then another is losing. There are so many good players out there, so you have to be really good to win big in poker.' Bruce describes himself as a 'solid player, a survivor. You can't play like them if you want to survive with a smaller stack.'

Ida Never Guessed

ON 30TH APRIL, 2016, IDA KEELING SET THE WORLD RECORD FOR THE 100-METRE SPRINT FOR CENTENARIANS, JUST A FEW WEEKS BEFORE HER 101ST BIRTHDAY.

She completed her feat during the masters mixed 80-and-older division race at the Penn Relays, the oldest and largest track and field competition in the United States, hosted annually since 1895 by the University of Pennsylvania at Franklin Field in Philadelphia.

The race was won by 88-year-old Ed Cox in 17.85 seconds, but Ida, who is barely 4 foot 6 and weighs 83 pounds, had the crowd of 44,000 on its feet as she crossed the finish line in 1 minute, 17.33 seconds. After the race she did several push-ups and told spectators, 'It was wonderful, I'm very happy to offer all of this crowd a nice example of what you can do for yourself, and I thank God every day for my blessings.'

Her advice for others wanting to push the boundaries of what's possible at her age is: 'Love yourself, do what you have to do, not what you want to do, eat for nutrition not for taste and exercise at least once a day.'

Keeling, who grew up in Harlem, still holds the American record for women aged 95 to 99 years old in the 60-metre sprint dash with a time of 29.86 seconds.

Negatives Attract

Curious when she found two black-and-white negatives in a drawer, pensioner Barbara had them made into prints. She was pleasantly surprised to see they were of a younger, slimmer her taken on one of her first dates with her husband. When she showed him the photographs, his face lit up. 'Wow!' he said. 'It's my old Hillman!'

> YOU DO LIVE LONGER WITH BRAN, BUT YOU SPEND THE LAST 15 YEARS ON THE
>
> # TOILET.
>
> *Alan King*

THE ONLY REASON I WOULD TAKE UP JOGGING IS SO I COULD HEAR HEAVY BREATHING AGAIN.

Erma Bombeck

I KEEP FIT. EVERY MORNING, I DO A HUNDRED LAPS OF AN OLYMPIC-SIZED SWIMMING POOL – IN A SMALL MOTOR LAUNCH.

Peter Cook

Now We Are Sixty

When he'd turned 60, Graeme had taken a lot of good-natured ribbing from family and friends. So as his wife Kathryn's 60th birthday approached, he decided to get in some needling of his own. He sat her down, looked deep into her eyes, then said he had never made love to anyone who was over 60 years old. 'Oh, well, I have,' she deadpanned. 'It's not that great.'

> **NO MAN LOVES LIFE LIKE HE THAT'S GROWING OLD.**
>
> *Sophocles*

LIFE'S UNDER NO OBLIGATION TO GIVE US WHAT WE EXPECT.

Margaret Mitchell

FORGET PAST MISTAKES. FORGET FAILURES. FORGET EVERYTHING EXCEPT WHAT YOU ARE GOING TO DO NOW AND DO IT.

William Durant

Rivalry Never Dies

IN 2008, NEPALESE FORMER GURKHA, MIN BAHADUR SHERCHAN OF BHURUNG, TATOPANI, BECAME THE OLDEST MAN TO CLIMB MOUNT EVEREST, AT THE AGE OF 76.

Five years later he was beaten by Japanese climber Yuichiro Miura, who conquered the 8,850-metre (29,035ft) Himalayan peak aged 80 after recovering from heart surgery.

The same year Min Bahadur Sherchan was forced to abandon another attempt after developing chest problems at base camp and having to be airlifted off the mountain. Undeterred, he spent the next two years raising funds to claim back the record for Nepal (a climbing permit alone for the mountain costs more than £35,000), but he had to cancel a 2015 ascent due to the devastating earthquake that hit the region.

The continuing rivalry of the two octogenarians shows that ambition, pride and fierce competition need not dim with advancing years.

Pole Position

IN AUGUST 2004, THREE YEARS BEFORE HER DEATH, DOROTHY DAVENHILL HIRSCH (BORN 11TH MAY, 1915) FROM PORTLAND, OREGON REACHED THE NORTH POLE ABOARD THE RUSSIAN NUCLEAR ICE BREAKER YAMAL, AND AT 89 YEARS AND 109 DAYS, WAS DESIGNATED BY THE GUINNESS BOOK OF WORLD RECORDS AS THE OLDEST PERSON TO REACH THE NORTH POLE.

With temperatures plummeting to –43°C the North Pole is a tough environment, but Dorothy was a tough woman. She served in the US Women's Army Corps during World War II and dedicated many years of her life to volunteer work.

Reaching one of the poles appears on many a bucket list, but Dorothy didn't let her age get in the way of turning a dream into a reality. She showed that it is never too late to do what you want to do, and be who you want to be.

Photo Shock

When Gladys turned 99, her grandchildren took some photographs with their mobiles as she blew out the candles on her birthday cake. She took one look at the photos, winced and remarked, 'Good heavens. I look like I'm a hundred years old.'

MANY PEOPLE DIE AT 25 AND AREN'T BURIED UNTIL THEY ARE 75.

Max Frisch

I DO WISH I COULD TELL YOU MY AGE BUT IT'S IMPOSSIBLE. IT KEEPS CHANGING ALL THE TIME.

Greer Garson

I'VE BEEN TRYING FOR SOME TIME TO DEVELOP A LIFESTYLE THAT DOESN'T REQUIRE MY PRESENCE.

Gary Trudeau

You can't turn back the clock. But you can wind it up again.

Bonnie Prudden

Ageing seems to be the only available
way to live a long life.

Kitty O'Neill Collins

IF YOU WAKE UP IN THE MORNING THEN YOU'RE AHEAD FOR

THE DAY.

Mace Neufield

'WRINKLES SHOULD MERELY
INDICATE WHERE SMILES
HAVE BEEN.'

Mark Twain

AFTER A MAN PASSES 60,
HIS MISCHIEF IS MAINLY IN
HIS HEAD.

Washington Irving

Trailer Park Professor

WHEN DON WIBERG WAS 57, HE LOST HIS JOB, HIS MARRIAGE BROKE DOWN, AND HE LOST HIS HOUSE AND SAVINGS IN THE DIVORCE SETTLEMENT.

Of course, life was hard for a while, but since focusing on the simpler things and adopting a can-do attitude, he has enjoyed some of the happiest years of his life. His home is a trailer park in Santa Cruz and he believes he is living in paradise.

Don was Professor of Engineering and Applied Science in the Electrical Engineering Department at University of California, Los Angeles. He had money, respect and prestige. Then he was given early retirement after the university made some cutbacks.

After a costly divorce and a fruitless search for an equivalent job, he found himself living in a refuge centre for poor people. But instead of getting depressed, he embraced his new life. He lived like a student, playing beach volleyball and bridge, meeting new people and just hanging out. He had a succession of girlfriends and lived in the moment for about six years.

Finally, at the age of 63, he landed a new job teaching and researching at U.C. Santa Cruz. The professor with a PhD from Caltech moved into a trailer park and met Jane, who lived nearby. They have been together ever since. Gone is the struggle for money, status and material one-upmanship. These things have been replaced by a calm generosity of spirit which has helped him discover the things that really matter in life – loving companionship and deep contentment.

WHEN WE RECALL THE PAST, WE USUALLY FIND THAT IT IS THE SIMPLEST THING – NOT THE GREAT OCCASIONS – THAT IN RETROSPECT GIVE OFF THE GREATEST GLOW OF HAPPINESS.

Bob Hope

Not So Fragile Now

INCREDIBLE CALIFORNIAN PENSIONER GRETA PONTARELLI IS IN HER 60S, BUT HAS THE BODY AND FLEXIBILITY OF A WOMAN DECADES YOUNGER AFTER TAKING UP POLE DANCING TO HELP HER OSTEOPOROSIS.

In 2013 she discovered that she was suffering from the fragile bone disease: 'To strengthen my bones, I needed strenuous exercise, something that would involve lifting weights. But just weight-lifting is very boring. That's why I looked into pole dancing.'

But she didn't stop there. Not only has her health dramatically improved, but she now competes internationally, and even won first place in the 2014 Pole Sports World Championship in the masters age 50-plus category.

Greta had always been physically active and had already tried aerobics, weight training and martial arts, but pole arts challenged her physically and creatively – it was the whole package. She was by no means a natural, however. The first time she tried it she couldn't get up the pole, but she resolved, 'I'm going to keep doing this until I have a little victory.'

She made little gains, step by step, each small victory encouraging her further and inspiring her and those around her: 'Whatever your dream is, you can always reach some level of achievement. Do something every day to be a little bit better. Those little victories will keep you going.'

Blind Date

'How was your blind date?'

'Terrible! He showed up in a 1932 Rolls-Royce.'

'What's so terrible about that?'

'He was the original owner.'

IF YOU OBEY ALL THE RULES, YOU MISS ALL THE FUN.

Katharine Hepburn

YOU WERE BORN AN ORIGINAL. DON'T DIE A COPY.

John Mason

THE SECRET OF MY LONG LIFE? SWIM, DANCE A LITTLE, GO TO PARIS EVERY AUGUST, AND LIVE WITHIN WALKING DISTANCE OF TWO HOSPITALS.

Dr Horatio Luro

Bless Me Father

An elderly man went to confession and said to the priest, 'Father, I'm 80 years old, married, and I have four kids and 11 grandchildren. I started taking Viagra and last night I made love to two 18-year-old girls. Both of them. Twice.'

The priest intoned: 'Well, my son, when was the last time you were in confession?'

'Never, Father, I'm Jewish.'

'So why are you telling me?'

'Are you kidding? I'm telling everybody!'

I HOPE I NEVER GET SO OLD I GET RELIGIOUS.

Ingmar Bergman

IF I'M FEELING REALLY WILD I DON'T BOTHER FLOSSING BEFORE BEDTIME.

Judith Viorst

I CAN'T WAIT TO GET OLD ENOUGH TO RIDE IN ONE OF THOSE BUGGIES AT THE AIRPORT. WHIZZING PAST ALL THOSE POOR SODS ON THE LONG TREK TO THE DEPARTURE GATE. IT WILL MAKE BEING OLD WORTHWHILE.

Sean Needham

Senator Into Space

ON 29TH OCTOBER, 1998, WHILE STILL A SITTING DEMOCRATIC SENATOR, FORMER TEST PILOT AND MERCURY ASTRONAUT JOHN GLENN MADE HISTORY WHEN HE BECAME THE OLDEST PERSON TO FLY IN SPACE.

At the age of 77, he flew as the Payload Specialist on Discovery Space Shuttle Mission STS-95. The mission lasted for 9 days, 2 hours and 39 minutes, and Glenn received a ticker tape parade on his return, 36 years after his last trip into space.

The physical forces on the human body while being blasted into orbit required Glenn to be physically fit and able to withstand forces of up to 3g (three times the force of gravity on Earth). Some of the Mercury astronauts experienced peak forces of 11.6g during re-entry, so Glenn was well within his comfort zone, despite his advanced years. After all, he had clocked up more than 9,000 hours of flying time, with approximately 3,000 hours in jet aircraft, and in 1962 he had become the first American to orbit the Earth.

According to the New York Times, Glenn 'won his seat on the Shuttle flight by lobbying NASA for two years to fly as a human guinea pig for geriatric studies'. It was the perfect opportunity for NASA to make a comparative study of the effects of space flight on the same test subject, almost four decades apart.

Young At Heart

IN MAY 2009, 66-YEAR-OLD ELIZABETH ADENEY FROM SUFFOLK BECAME BRITAIN'S OLDEST MUM WHEN SHE GAVE BIRTH TO A SON.

She was childless and recently single when she underwent fertility treatment in the Ukraine using a donor egg and donor sperm. She gave birth by caesarean section at Addenbrooke's Hospital in Cambridge, beating the previous record holder, Patti Farrant, who had her son JJ at the age of 62 three years earlier. She too had undergone IVF treatment abroad using a donated egg, as clinics in the UK refuse to treat women over 50.

Elizabeth named her 5lb 3oz baby Jolyon, which means 'young at heart'. Defending her decision to have a child at her age, she said, 'It's not physical age that is important – it's how I feel inside. Some days I feel 39. Others, I feel 56.'

Four weeks after giving birth, Elizabeth resumed working a five-day week at the Suffolk plastics and textiles firm where she was managing director, placing her son in the care of a nanny.

IF WE TAKE CARE OF THE MOMENTS, THE YEARS WILL TAKE CARE OF THEMSELVES.

Maria Edgeworth

Two For One

Just before the funeral service, the undertaker came up to the very elderly widow and asked, 'How old was your husband?'

'98,' she replied. 'Two years older than me.'

'So you're 96,' the undertaker commented.

She responded, 'Hardly worth going home, is it?'

IF I HAD MY LIFE TO LIVE OVER AGAIN, I'D MAKE THE SAME MISTAKES –

ONLY SOONER.

Tallulah Bankhead

AT FIFTY, THE MADWOMAN IN THE ATTIC BREAKS LOOSE, STOMPS DOWN THE STAIRS, AND SETS FIRE TO THE HOUSE. SHE WON'T BE IMPRISONED ANYMORE.

Erica Jong

IF I HAD MY LIFE TO LIVE OVER AGAIN ... I WOULD HAVE SAT ON THE LAWN WITH MY CHILDREN AND NOT WORRIED ABOUT GRASS STAINS.

Erma Bombeck

Old people do more scandalous things than any rebel
you want to name. Because they don't give a damn.
They couldn't give a rat's ass what you think ... They're leaving
soon, you know what I mean?

Chris Isaak

DIPLOMAT: A MAN WHO REMEMBERS A WOMAN'S BIRTHDAY
BUT FORGETS HER AGE.

NEVER REGRET. IF IT'S GOOD, IT'S WONDERFUL. IT IT'S BAD, IT'S

EXPERIENCE.

Victoria Holt

THE OTHER NIGHT I SAID TO MY WIFE RUTH, 'DO YOU FEEL THAT
THE SEX AND EXCITEMENT HAVE GONE OUT OF OUR MARRIAGE?'
SHE SAID, 'I'LL DISCUSS IT WITH YOU DURING THE
NEXT COMMERCIAL.'

Milton Berle

Gift From God

IN 2010, RAYMOND CALVERT BECAME THE UK'S OLDEST NEW DAD AT 78 AFTER FATHERING A 7LB 1OZ BABY SON WITH A 25-YEAR-OLD WOMAN.

Raymond had already had six children, raising some of them as a single parent after his wife died 28 years earlier. They ranged in age from 38 to 51 and he also had nine grandchildren. He first met Charlotte after having a three-year relationship with her mum.

Unsurprisingly, news of the planned pregnancy sent shockwaves through the family, and created a rift with those who felt betrayed and sickened by their apparent deception, including his grown-up children. But Raymond was immune to any criticism and dismissed it as jealousy. He told reporters: 'He's a gift from God – my very own little miracle.' The former market trader also declared his intention to remain faithful to the young mother: 'There was no bigger womaniser than me, but now I'm true to Charlotte.'

Charlotte praised her pensioner beau: 'I realised it would be nice to have a baby Raymond. He has such a lot of nice qualities. I knew he'd be a great dad as he's done such a good job with his own children.'

Still Practising

LEILA DENMARK WAS AN AMERICAN PAEDIATRICIAN IN ATLANTA, GEORGIA, AND THE WORLD'S OLDEST PRACTISING DOCTOR UNTIL HER RETIREMENT IN MAY 2001 AT THE AGE OF 103.

Leila started treating children in 1928. When she retired she was treating the grandchildren and great-grandchildren of her first patients.

Born in Portal, Georgia, in 1898, the third of 12 children, Leila initially trained to be a teacher but decided to attend medical school (where she was the only woman in her class) after her fiancé John was posted to Java in the Dutch Indies by the US Department of State. Women were not allowed to accompany their husbands, so she busied herself by becoming only the third woman ever to graduate from the Medical College of Georgia in Augusta with a medical degree.

During a career that spanned 73 years she was a pioneer in the treatment of whooping cough and she is credited with developing the vaccine that has saved thousands of young lives. In 1971 she published a parenting book called Every Child Should Have a Chance. She was one of the first doctors to call for parents to stop smoking around children and she was an early adopter of the idea that cow's milk and fruit juices can be harmful.

After her retirement she lived for another eleven years. At her death in April 2012 she was the fifth oldest verified living person in the world.

KEEP SETTING GOALS AND DREAMING DREAMS.
DON'T RETIRE – RETREAD.

I've always felt that it was important to not only accept it,
but in a sense to revere the process of
getting older.

Emma Thompson

People mature with age and experience.
I hope I more resemble a fine wine than bad vinegar.

Rick Kaplan

FOR YEARS I WANTED TO BE OLDER, AND

NOW I AM.

Margaret Atwood

NOTHING IS REALLY WORK UNLESS YOU WOULD RATHER BE DOING SOMETHING ELSE.

James M. Barrie

Prime Plot

An elderly couple were making their funeral arrangements. The young cemetery salesman pointed out a double plot that he thought they would like.

'You'll have a beautiful view of the Somerset Levels,' he assured them.

The old man wasn't keen: 'Unless you're including a periscope with our coffins, I don't know how you expect us to enjoy it.'

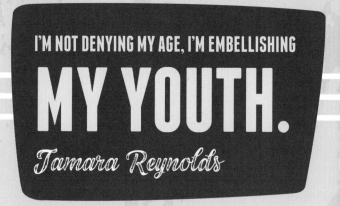

I'M NOT DENYING MY AGE, I'M EMBELLISHING

MY YOUTH.

Tamara Reynolds

NEVER THINK YOU'VE SEEN THE LAST OF ANYTHING.

Eudora Welty

BE EQUAL TO YOUR TALENT, NOT YOUR AGE. AT TIMES LET THE GAP BETWEEN THEM BE EMBARRASSING.

Yevgeny Yevtushenko

Gnarly Old Dude

LLOYD KAHN FIRST TRIED SKATEBOARDING AT 65. HE FELL OFF ALMOST IMMEDIATELY AND REALISED HE NEEDED TO INVEST IN SOME PROTECTIVE EQUIPMENT.

After purchasing a helmet, elbow and knee pads, and gloves with hockey pucks on the palms, Lloyd got right back on his board and was still enjoying regular downhill long-board skating around the San Francisco area fifteen years later.

Interviewed at the age of 76, he said, 'The thing about learning a new physical skill when you're older, I think it's good for your brain. I always try to do something physical every day or I don't feel very well.' But he doesn't do any special tricks: 'I don't ride like the teenagers. I try not to go too fast, so that I could always jump off and land on my feet.'

Lloyd decided to finally hang up his skateboard at the age of 80 on Sunday, 6th December, 2015, after a fall. The next day he wrote about the decision on his blog: 'Busted! Compound fracture of my wrist, that is. It happened just when skating was going so good … But in the back of my mind, I promised myself to quit if I ever had a serious crash.'

With no regrets, he stays active and continues his main passion as founding editor-in-chief of Shelter Publications, Inc., which among other things publishes fitness books, and as a pioneer of the green building and green architecture movements.

Little House in the Big Woods

LAURA INGALLS WILDER WAS THE AMERICAN WRITER OF THE LITTLE HOUSE ON THE PRAIRIE SERIES OF CHILDREN'S NOVELS, BASED ON HER CHILDHOOD. THE FIRST BOOK WAS PUBLISHED WHEN SHE WAS 65 YEARS OLD AND THE LAST ONE HIT THE SHELVES WHEN SHE WAS 76.

Born in 1867, she grew up in a series of log cabins and homesteads in the Big Woods of Wisconsin, Missouri, Kansas, Lake City, Minnesota and South Troy, Minnesota. Following a brief stint as a school teacher in a one-room school, she married 28-year-old Almanzo Wilder, set up home and eked out an existence, weathering a storm of troubles, which included her husband's partial paralysis from diphtheria, the death of their newborn son, their house burning down and several years of drought. They then moved to a farmstead in Mansfield, Missouri, which finally bore the fruits of their labour after twenty years of back-breaking toil.

In 1911, then in her forties, Laura became a columnist with a local newspaper and started to hone her craft and enjoy a stable living, but as she reached her retirement, the stock market crash of 1929 wiped out the family savings. Laura began writing in earnest by necessity. Once again, hardship and misfortune were the making of her: Little House in the Big Woods was published in 1932, when she was 65, and she went on to publish another seven volumes in the series, as a record of pioneering life in the late nineteenth century.

> ## NO ONE GROWS OLD BY LIVING – ONLY BY LOSING INTEREST IN LIVING.
>
> *Marie Ray*

All my friends are dead. They're all in heaven now and they're all up there mingling with one another. By now, they are starting to wonder if I might have gone to the other place.

Teresa Platt

I don't look my age, I don't feel my age and I don't act my age.

Joan Collins

YOU LIVE LONGER ONCE YOU REALISE THAT ANY TIME SPENT BEING UNHAPPY

IS WASTED.

Ruth E. Renkl

MY GRANDFATHER IS HARD OF HEARING. HE NEEDS TO READ LIPS. I DON'T MIND HIM READING LIPS, BUT HE USES ONE OF THOSE YELLOW HIGHLIGHTERS.

Brian Kiley

Hipster Chic

'What's a hipster?' four-year-old Johnny asked his mother.

'Someone who wears something just to look different,' she replied. 'They often wear clothes from charity shops and have thick glasses.'

'Is Grandma a hipster?' he asked.

TO LENGTHEN THY LIFE, LESSEN THY MEALS.

Benjamin Franklin

I HAVE A SIMPLE PHILOSOPHY: FILL WHAT'S EMPTY. EMPTY WHAT'S FULL. AND SCRATCH WHERE IT ITCHES.

Eudora Welty

WHENEVER I'M CONFUSED, I JUST CHECK MY UNDERWEAR. IT HOLDS THE ANSWER TO ALL THE IMPORTANT QUESTIONS.

Grampa Simpson, The Simpsons

Late Starter

FAUJA SINGH IS A BRITISH MARATHON RUNNER OF PUNJABI INDIAN DESCENT, AND HE HOLDS ALL THE WORLD RECORDS IN HIS AGE GROUP. SINCE TAKING UP RUNNING, AGED 89, HE HAS RUN NINE FULL MARATHONS.

At the age of 92 he set the over-90s marathon record of 5 hours 40 minutes at the Toronto Waterfront Marathon and at the same event eight years later in 2011 he became the first centenarian to finish a marathon.

Singh retired from competitive races in February 2013 at the age of 102 after completing a 10K race in Hong Kong, but his retirement didn't last – he competed in the Mumbai marathon in 2016 at the age of 104! Like many who discover running late in life, his motivation for running was to deal with bereavement: 'It was God's way of distracting me from suffering mentally from the loss of my wife and son.'

He follows a basic Punjabi vegetarian diet, with plenty of fresh fruit and vegetables, but he also restricts his calories, consuming what would generally be described as child portions. He also enjoys a ginger curry at least once a week to cleanse the body. As a result of his diet and exercise regime, at the age of 105 he shows no sign of heart disease and he needs no medication.

Turning Over Every Stone

AN 82-YEAR-OLD RETIRED TEACHER FROM WALES RECENTLY ENTERED THE GUINNESS BOOK OF WORLD RECORDS AS THE OLDEST FEMALE SKYDIVER EVER, AND HER RECORD-BREAKING DIVE WASN'T JUST A ONE-OFF – SHE'S CLOCKED UP 1,132 JUMPS OVER NEARLY THIRTY YEARS.

Pensioner Dilys Price can think of nothing more enjoyable than 'jumping out of an aeroplane and going: "Yeeesss!" I love it. I need it. I can't imagine life without it.'

She made her first jump when she was 54 and was instantly hooked, even though she used to be scared of heights. She believes her passion for skydiving keeps her young at heart and healthy. Her key to a long productive life is: 'turning over every stone, until underneath you find something you're passionate about'.

She remembers her first tandem jump like it was yesterday. She felt sick and thought she was going to die, but her fear quickly changed to exhilaration as she flew through the air, strapped to her instructor. As soon as she reached the ground she knew she wanted to learn how to skydive solo, but at first her local skydiving club was unsure whether she was already too old to learn to dive safely. Fortunately they relented and now Dilys is an octogenarian record-breaker.

Dressed to Impress

Doris: Whenever I'm down in the dumps,
I get myself a new outfit.

Flo: Really? I wondered where you got them from.

ONCE I REALISED HOW EXPENSIVE FUNERALS ARE, I BEGAN TO EXERCISE AND WATCH MY DIET.

Thomas Sowell

YEARS GROW SHORTER BUT DAYS GROW LONGER. WHEN YOU'RE OVER 70, A DAY IS AN AWFUL LOT OF TIME.

Carl Sandburg

WHEN ONE SUBTRACTS FROM LIFE INFANCY (WHICH IS VEGETATION), SLEEP, EATING AND SWILLING, BUTTONING AND UNBUTTONING – HOW MUCH REMAINS OF DOWNRIGHT EXISTENCE? THE SUMMER OF A DORMOUSE.

Yevgeny Yevtushenko

Lines Crossed

Three old guys are out walking.

The first one says, 'Windy, isn't it?'

The second one says, 'No, it's Thursday!'

The third one says, 'So am I. Let's go for a beer.'

THE FIRST TIME I SEE A JOGGER SMILING, I'LL CONSIDER IT.

Joan Rivers

I GET MY EXERCISE RUNNING TO THE FUNERALS OF MY FRIENDS WHO EXERCISE.

Barry Gray

I'VE EXERCISED WITH WOMEN SO THIN THAT BUZZARDS FOLLOWED THEM TO THEIR CARS.

Erma Bombeck

Late Finisher

NOLA OCHS IS THE WORLD'S OLDEST COLLEGE GRADUATE. SHE TOOK HER FIRST COLLEGE COURSE AT FORT HAYS STATE UNIVERSITY IN 1930 – BUT DIDN'T FINISH HER DEGREE UNTIL 2007, AT THE AGE OF 95.

On 14th May, 2007, Ochs received her diploma at FHSU in general studies with an emphasis in history. She graduated alongside her granddaughter, Alexandra Ochs, who was 21 years old. Then she continued with her education and completed a master's degree in liberal studies, which she received from FHSU in May 2010 at the age of 98.

While studying, she set her sights on becoming a storyteller on a cruise ship. After graduating, she became a minor celebrity and even appeared on The Tonight Show with Jay Leno. Soon afterwards, Princess Cruises hired her as a guest lecturer on a nine-day Caribbean cruise. As she celebrated her 100th birthday in November 2011, she was continuing to take further master's-level classes and was working as a graduate teaching assistant.

'I don't dwell on my age. It might limit what I can do. As long as I have my mind and health, age is just a number.'

Varicoloured Varley

IN 1999, 61-YEAR-OLD ISOBEL VARLEY FROM STEVENAGE, HERTFORDSHIRE ENTERED THE GUINNESS BOOK OF WORLD RECORDS AS THE MOST TATTOOED FEMALE SENIOR CITIZEN AFTER SPENDING MORE THAN 500 HOURS BEING INKED.

The married mother-of-one, who grew up in Yorkshire, got her first tattoo in 1986, when she was 49, after being inspired by attending a tattoo convention at the Hammersmith Palais: 'I was so impressed by the sheer beauty of the tattoos and I found that the people there were ordinary people from all walks of life and were not strange.'

Her favourite tattoo was a family of tigers on her stomach and she also had about 50 piercings, including 29 in her ears, two in her nose, one through each nipple and 16 in her nether regions.

The only areas not completely tattooed were her face, the soles of her feet, her ears and some parts of her hands. By the time of her death in 2015, 93 per cent of her body was inked: 'Originally, I was only ever going to have one – a small bird – but I fell in love with it, and developed an addiction.' Isobel spent about £20,000 in total on her body art, but in her later years she didn't pay for new tattoos because people wanted to tattoo her.

BEAUTIFUL YOUNG PEOPLE ARE ACCIDENTS OF NATURE, BUT BEAUTIFUL OLD PEOPLE ARE WORKS OF ART.

Eleanor Roosevelt

The great secret that all old people share is that you really haven't changed in 70 or 80 years. Your body changes, but you don't change at all. And that, of course, causes great confusion.

Doris Lessing

THEY SAY THAT AGE IS ALL IN YOUR MIND. THE TRICK IS TO KEEP IT FROM CREEPING DOWN INTO YOUR BODY.

I AM REALLY LOOKING FORWARD, AS I GET OLDER AND OLDER, TO BEING LESS AND

LESS NICE.

Annette Bening

MOISTURISERS DO WORK. THE REST IS PAP. THERE IS NOTHING ON GOD'S EARTH THAT WILL TAKE AWAY 30 YEARS OF ARGUING WITH YOUR HUSBAND.

Anita Roddick

I Remember Her When

A 35-year-old woman was walking with her elderly mother when they ran into an old family acquaintance. 'Is this your daughter?' the woman asked of the older lady. 'Oh, I remember her when she was little. How old is she now?'

Without blinking the mother replied, 'Twenty-four.'

After she had gone, the young woman confronted her mother. 'Why did you take eleven years off me?'

'Well,' she replied, 'I've been lying about my age for so long, it suddenly dawned on me that I'd have to start lying about yours too.'

FEW PEOPLE KNOW HOW TO BE OLD.

François de La Rochefoucauld

AGE IS NOT A PARTICULARLY INTERESTING SUBJECT. ANYONE CAN GET OLD. ALL YOU HAVE TO DO IS LIVE LONG ENOUGH.

Groucho Marx

Oldest Living Person

ON 13TH MAY, 2016, 116-YEAR-OLD EMMA MORANO BECAME THE WORLD'S OLDEST LIVING PERSON, THE OLDEST-EVER ITALIAN AND ONE OF THE TEN VERIFIED OLDEST PEOPLE EVER.

She is also the last verified living person born in the 1800s. She was born on 29th November, 1899 in Civiasco, Piedmont, Italy, the eldest of eight children. When she was young a doctor advised her family to move somewhere with a healthy climate, so they moved to Pallanza, on Lake Maggiore, where she still lives.

In 2011 she was awarded the Knight of Order of Merit of the Italian Republic by President Giorgio Napolitano, and five years later, when she turned 116, she was congratulated by Pope Francis.

She attributes her longevity to several factors: she has never used drugs, she drinks a glass of homemade brandy every day and enjoys chocolate occasionally, but the three most important things are eating three raw eggs daily, being positive about the future and remaining single (she claims to have kicked her abusive husband out of the house in 1938, although they remained married until his death in 1978).

On 29th July, 2016 she was presented with a certificate from Guinness World Records confirming her status as the oldest person alive.

Porridge But No Oats

ON 2ND JANUARY, 2015, JESSIE CALLAN, THE OLDEST WOMAN IN SCOTLAND, CELEBRATED HER 109TH BIRTHDAY IN A CARE HOME IN ABERDEEN AND DECLARED THAT THE SECRET TO A LONG LIFE IS PLENTY OF PORRIDGE AND NO MEN.

News of her birthday went viral and she had people phoning her from across the world and even coming to the front door to pass on their good wishes.

Born in 1906, Jessie grew up in a tiny two-room farm cottage in Kintore, on the banks of the River Don in Aberdeenshire, which she shared with her parents, five sisters and one brother. She recalled: 'We never had any money, but we were all very happy.'

She spent a decade working as a waitress at the Lauriston Hotel in Ballater, where she claimed the visit of Queen Elizabeth and the Queen Mother was the highlight of each year.

Her secret to a long life was staying away from men: 'They're just more trouble than they're worth. I also made sure that I got plenty of exercise, eat a nice warm bowl of porridge every morning and have never got married.'

Can You Keep A Secret?

Helen Mirren had laryngitis and decided to go to see a top Hollywood throat specialist. After the nurse called for her, she asked her age.

'Seventy-one,' whispered the dame.

'Don't worry,' the nurse whispered back. 'I won't tell anyone.'

GETTING OLD IS A FASCINATING THING.
THE OLDER YOU GET, THE OLDER YOU WANT

TO GET.

Keith Richards

IF I'D KNOWN I WAS GONNA LIVE THIS LONG, I'D HAVE TAKEN BETTER CARE OF MYSELF.

Eubie Blake

TURNING 100 WAS THE WORST BIRTHDAY OF MY LIFE. I WOULDN'T WISH IT ON MY WORST ENEMY. TURNING 101 WAS NOT SO BAD. ONCE YOU'RE PAST THAT CENTURY MARK, IT'S JUST NOT SHOCKING.

Erma Bombeck

Develop your eccentricities while you are young. That way, when you get old, people won't think you're going gaga.

David Ogilvy

Whenever I feel like exercise, I lie down until the feeling passes.

R.M. Hutchins

YOU DON'T CROSS A FRONTIER TO OLD AGE – YOU JUST SIMPLY GO ON

BEING YOU.

Joan Bakewell

ETERNITY IS NOT SOMETHING THAT BEGINS AFTER YOU ARE DEAD. IT IS GOING ON ALL THE TIME.

Charlotte Perkins Gilman

Danseur Nobbly

IN AUGUST 2009, JOHN LOWE, A 90-YEAR-OLD WAR VETERAN, BECAME BRITAIN'S OLDEST BALLET DANCER WHEN HE STARRED IN STRAUSS'S AN ARTIST'S LIFE WITH THE LANTERN DANCE THEATRE COMPANY AT ELY CATHEDRAL IN CAMBRIDGESHIRE.

He only took up ballet at the age of 79 (inspired by his daughter Alison who is a professional dancer), but eleven years later he still maintained his fitness by practising three times a week, and hung from a trapeze on his living room ceiling every morning to increase his strength.

The father of four and grandfather of 11, who was captured by the Japanese in the Second World War and nearly died from hard labour and starvation, celebrated being alive by doing what he loved: 'You have to be incredibly fit and I see these people crawling around, hunched over smoking a cigarette. They should be doing ballet. Dancing is the most amazing feeling and you come home mentally uplifted after listening to all this brilliant music.'

Interviewed five years later, he was still dancing and explained its lasting attraction at 94: 'It is a joy to move to beautiful music. But the really important thing for me is that I am working with much younger people who treat me not as an old man – which I most certainly am – but as a friend.'

THE TRICK IS GROWING UP WITHOUT GROWING OLD.

Casey Stengel

Living Without Money

RETIRED GERMAN PSYCHOTHERAPIST HEIDEMARIE SCHWERMER LIVED FOR TWO DECADES WITHOUT MONEY.

When she was 53, Heidemarie began an experiment that would change her life. She moved out of her rented apartment, and gave away almost all of her belongings and all her money, apart from 200 Euros, which she saved for an emergency fund. She never used it. Her only belongings in the world were a change of clothes, three pairs of shoes, glasses and some make-up.

She began her new life by staying with friends in return for free psychotherapy, but having a live-in therapist didn't prove as popular as she had imagined. Undeterred, she turned to manual labour to repay the hospitality of her hosts: cleaning windows, babysitting, or doing gardening and other odd jobs in exchange for room and board.

As word spread of her unusual lifestyle choice, she found herself in demand all over the world to appear on television and give speeches at conferences. In each case, travel, accommodation and food were provided free in exchange for her lived wisdom: 'It's believed that money is the key that opens all doors. I am now convinced that love and trust can also be used as that key.'

> IT IS BETTER TO LIVE RICH THAN TO DIE RICH.
> *Samuel Johnson*

Ice Cream, You Scream

A little old man shuffled into an ice cream parlour and pulled himself slowly, painfully, up onto a stool. After catching his breath, he ordered a knickerbocker glory.

The waitress asked, 'Crushed nuts?'

'No,' he replied. 'Arthritis.'

SOMETIMES YOU HAVE TO MAKE A DECISION TO BE HAPPY.

Olympia Dukakis

YOU GOT TO BE CAREFUL IF YOU DON'T KNOW WHERE YOU'RE GOING, BECAUSE YOU MIGHT NOT GET THERE.

Yogi Berra

YOU DON'T HAVE TO BE RICH AND FAMOUS. YOU JUST HAVE TO BE AN ORDINARY PERSON, DOING EXTRAORDINARY THINGS.

Joan Armatrading

If you keep working you'll last longer and I just want to keep vertical. I'd hate to spend the rest of my life trying to outwit an 18-inch fish.

Harold S. Geneen

If you live to be 100 you've got it made – very few people die past that age.

George Burns

A MAN OF 60 HAS SPENT 20 YEARS IN BED AND OVER THREE YEARS IN
EATING.

Arnold Bennett

IN THE DAYS WHEN I WENT TO WORK, I NEVER ONCE KNEW WHAT I WAS DOING. THESE DAYS, I NEVER WORK. WORK DOES AGE ONE SO.

Quentin Crisp

Jiro Dreams of Sushi

JIRO ONO IS A JAPANESE CHEF AND OWNER OF SUKIYABASHI JIRO, A THREE-MICHELIN-STARRED SUSHI RESTAURANT IN TOKYO.

Not only does Jiro Ono hold the Guinness World Record for the oldest living chef, but he is widely considered to be the greatest living sushi chef in the world. His tiny restaurant only seats ten people and it is located in a Tokyo subway station, where prices start at 30,000 Japanese yen (about £230) for a tasting menu of 20 courses. Visitors have to book six weeks in advance to dine there.

In 2011 Jiro was the star of the documentary film Jiro Dreams of Sushi, directed by the American filmmaker David Gelb, filmed when the chef was 85 years old. Originally, Gelb had planned to make a film about several different sushi chefs around the world, but he was so captivated by Jiro's brilliance, his quest for perfection and his relationship with his two middle-aged sons – who are also sushi chefs – that he decided to focus entirely on Jiro and his family.

'I do the same thing over and over, improving bit by bit,' says Jiro. 'There is always a yearning to achieve more. I will continue to climb, trying to reach the top – but no one knows where the top is … I love making sushi … I've never once hated this job. I fell in love with my work and gave my life to it.'

Shredded Shepherd

UNTIL THE AGE OF 56, FORMER BALTIMORE SCHOOL ADMINISTRATOR ERNESTINE SHEPHERD WAS A SELF-CONFESSED 'COUCH POTATO'.

Now in her eighties, she has run nine marathons, can bench press more than her own weight, has six-pack abs and has entered the Guinness Book of World Records as the oldest competitive female bodybuilder.

She wakes at 2.30am, says her prayers and eats ten scrambled egg whites and a handful of walnuts, washed down with sixteen ounces of water. Then she goes for a ten-mile jog in the dark with a head torch. She runs 80 miles a week and performs bicep curls with 20-pound dumbbells. She spends her days lifting weights and running fitness classes for other senior citizens at the Union Memorial Methodist Church in Baltimore.

Her wake-up call came when she and her sister Mildred were trying on swimsuits during their mid-fifties. They didn't like what they saw in the mirror, so they started aerobics classes together and resolved to become the fittest seniors in existence. When Mildred died suddenly from a brain aneurysm, Ernestine vowed to continue the quest alone, in tribute to her memory. 'I kept up everything she said we were going to do. That's kept me so close to her.'

It's hard to be devil-may-care when there are
pleats in your derrière.

Judith Viorst

You can't help getting older, but you can help yourself from
becoming old and infirm, in mind as well as body.

Joan Collins

I KNOW I CAN'T CHEAT DEATH, BUT I CAN CHEAT

OLD AGE.

Darwin Deason

I HAVE THE BODY OF AN 18-YEAR-OLD.
I KEEP IT IN THE FRIDGE.

Spike Milligan

Shine A Light

A care assistant asked one of her clients, a retired vicar, whether he was having any senior issues. 'Well,' replied the old man, 'I suffer from a weak bladder and poor eyesight, so I used to wet my bed. But now I'm happy to go to the bathroom during the night, because the Lord in his infinite mercy turns on the light as soon as I open the door.'

'Ah, that solves a mystery,' replied the care assistant. 'So it's you who keeps peeing in the fridge.'

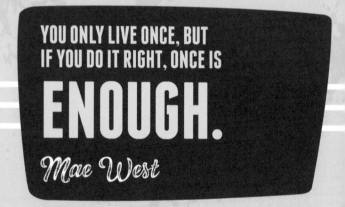

YOU ONLY LIVE ONCE, BUT IF YOU DO IT RIGHT, ONCE IS

ENOUGH.

Mae West

THERE IS A VERY FINE LINE BETWEEN 'HOBBY' AND 'MENTAL ILLNESS'.

Dave Barry

LIFE ISN'T MEASURED BY HOW MANY BREATHS WE TAKE, BUT BY THE MOMENTS THAT TAKE OUR BREATH AWAY.

Chinese saying

Double Out and Back

A PAIR OF THRILL-SEEKING PENSIONERS FROM CORNWALL HAVE SPENT OVER £60,000 INDULGING THEIR MUTUAL PASSION FOR RIDING ROLLERCOASTERS.

Dennis and Sylvia Bloor from Tregurrian, near Newquay, are the oldest members of the Rollercoaster Club of Great Britain. They have ridden their favourite rollercoaster – Nemesis at Alton Towers – nearly 4,000 times in the last 20 years and have spent their retirement travelling the world in search of bigger and faster rides, clocking up more than 250 rides in more than 40 theme parks across Europe and North America.

Interviewed in 2013, Sylvia extolled the health benefits: 'Everybody's always telling us we look so youthful; I tell them it's all the screaming we do. It's all about the adrenaline, the fun and the anticipation. I've got arthritis and it's like having a cortisone injection.'

For years, the former BT workers had lived just a few miles from Alton Towers, but they only paid their first visit shortly before moving to Cornwall. After discovering Nemesis they were hooked and now travel back there up to 20 times a year. 'Who needs booze or anything like that when you have this?' says Dennis. 'It's all about the exhilaration, the fresh air, and above all, the fun. We love it.'

Grandma Moses

ANNA MARY ROBERTSON MOSES WAS A FAMOUS AMERICAN FOLK ARTIST WHO CREATED MORE THAN 1,500 CANVASSES DURING HER PROLIFIC 25-YEAR CAREER.

Her homely pastoral landscapes hang in museums around the world. She appeared on magazine covers, her paintings appeared on postage stamps, she was the subject of a documentary of her life, she received two honorary doctorates and she penned her autobiography. But she didn't pick up a paintbrush until her late seventies. She only switched from embroidery to painting because arthritis had made needlework too painful.

'Grandma Moses' sprung to fame after a New York art collector, Louis Calder, spotted her work in a drug store window in Hoosick Falls in 1938 and bought several of her paintings. The following year, when she was nearly 80, three of her paintings appeared in an exhibition at the Museum of Modern Art in New York called 'Contemporary Unknown American Painters'. Today many of her paintings sell for seven-figure sums. 'Sugaring Off' sold for $1.2 million in 2006.

Grandma Moses painted scenes of rural America from her early life, to record the past for future generations. Her creative process was disarmingly simple: '[I'll] get an inspiration and start painting; then I'll forget everything, everything except how things used to be and how to paint it so people will know how we used to live.'

> IF A WOMAN IS SUFFICIENTLY AMBITIOUS, DETERMINED AND GIFTED – THERE IS PRACTICALLY NOTHING SHE CAN'T DO.
>
> *Helen Lawrenson*

I am delighted to find that even at my age great ideas come to me, the pursuit and development of which should require another lifetime.

Johann Wolfgang von Goethe

Who would be young in age, must in youth be sage.

German proverb

AS I GET OLDER THE YEARS JUST FLY BY. I DON'T THINK THERE WAS AN APRIL

THIS YEAR.

Jeremy Hardy

ONE DAY, AGED 45, I JUST WENT INTO THE KITCHEN TO MAKE MYSELF A CUP OF TEA, AND WHEN I CAME OUT I FOUND I WAS 68.

Thora Hird

Nobody really talks to old people, cos, you know, you don't know what they're saying. They just go, 'Arghh, arghh, arghh,' and you don't know if they're having a good time or being bitten.

Dylan Moran

YOU KNOW YOU'RE OLD WHEN IT TAKES YOU TWICE AS LONG TO LOOK HALF AS GOOD.

THE OLDER I GET THE BETTER I

USED TO BE.

Lee Trevino

I THINK ONE OF THE REASONS THAT I'VE LASTED AS LONG AS I HAVE – TOUCH WOOD – IS THAT I'M NO BOTHER.

June Whitfield

Tiantan Park Therapy

BY THE TIME HE RETIRED, DUAN TZINFU COULD BARELY WALK OR BREATHE AFTER SPENDING 50 YEARS WORKING IN A GLASS FACTORY.

But Duan's life changed the day he walked through Tiantan, a Beijing city park, and spotted a group of people exercising in the open air. Tiantan Park, or Temple of Heaven Park, is world famous for its morning activities and as a social venue, where hundreds of people gather very early to take part in one of the scores of free exercise groups.

Duan was impressed by the enthusiasm and flexibility of the people exercising, not to mention the fact that many of them were much older than him. They could do the splits with ease, while he could barely bend over without wheezing in pain.

Duan joined a group which performed stretching and relaxation exercises and practised techniques based on Daoist principles. He turned up every day, just as he had turned up for work every day, only this time he was restoring his health rather than destroying it. Little by little he regained strength and balance, and is now so flexible that he can wrap his legs round his back with ease – and do the splits. 'It's important to stretch and to eat less tasty foods,' he maintains. 'Then, you'll be healthy and happy.'

Big Spray

FRANCES WOOFENDEN STARTED WATER-SKIING WHEN SHE MOVED TO FLORIDA AT THE AGE OF 50. BY THE TIME SHE HIT HER MID-EIGHTIES, SHE HAD COLLECTED SCORES OF MEDALS FOR COMPETITIVE TRICK WATER-SKIING.

She even became the face of V8, the vegetable drink, performing a host of front-to-back and back-to-front tricks at 28 mph, during an eight-hour shoot for their television commercial. 'I never even think about my age,' she said, 'until my birthday rolls around and I see all those candles.'

Frances chose water-skiing because she wanted to try something fun and active that would boost her health and keep her feeling young. She persuaded her husband, Stewart, to buy a ski towboat after admiring the elegance of a young girl she saw skiing. The 4-foot-10 and 95-pound athlete often takes to the water wearing a brightly coloured backless swimsuit, gold earrings and hot pink lipstick. When a CBS News correspondent expressed surprise, on national television, at the West Palm Beach grandmother's appearance, she replied, 'What was I going to wear, bloomers?'

When she isn't wowing everybody on the water, Frances likes to teach the younger skiers how to knit. She also bicycles ten miles a day and kayaks around the nearby freshwater Lake Osborne.

I have never seen an old person in a new bathing suit in my life. I don't know where they get their bathing suits, but my father has bathing suits from other centuries. If I forget mine, he always wants me to wear his.

Jerry Seinfeld

THE OLDER A MAN GETS, THE FARTHER HE HAD TO WALK TO SCHOOL AS A BOY.

ONE STARTS TO GET YOUNG AT THE AGE OF 60 AND THEN IT IS

TOO LATE.

Pablo Picasso

I THINK ALL THIS TALK ABOUT AGE IS FOOLISH.
EVERY TIME I'M ONE YEAR OLDER,
EVERYONE ELSE IS TOO.

Gloria Swanson

If you wake up in your pyjamas – it's morning.
If you're in your clothes – it's time for tea.

Thora Hird

The old believe everything, the middle-aged suspect
everything, the young know everything.

Oscar Wilde

I DON'T WANT TO RETIRE. I'M NOT THAT GOOD AT CROSSWORD PUZZLES.

Norman Mailer

YOU WILL DIE NOT BECAUSE YOU ARE ILL.
YOU WILL DIE BECAUSE YOU ARE ALIVE.

Seneca

To Reach The Unreachable

MIGUEL DE CERVANTES IS WIDELY REGARDED AS THE GREATEST WRITER IN THE SPANISH LANGUAGE BUT HE DIDN'T COMPLETE THE SECOND PART OF HIS SEMINAL WORK AND THE BESTSELLING BOOK OF ALL TIME, DON QUIXOTE, UNTIL MONTHS BEFORE HIS DEATH, AT THE AGE OF 68.

Born in 1547, he grew up in a poor household with little stability, as the family moved from town to town. In his youth he fell in love with a barmaid and they planned to elope, but the union was scuppered by her father, because the young Miguel had such poor prospects.

In his early twenties he enlisted as a soldier in a regiment of the Spanish Navy Marines. He was severely injured at the Battle of Lepanto and lost the use of his left hand. He was later taken captive by Ottoman pirates and spent five years as a slave in Algiers before being ransomed and returning home to Madrid.

He spent the next twenty years leading a nomadic existence as a purchasing agent for the Spanish Armada and as a tax collector. During this time he was imprisoned at least twice for financial irregularities. He published his first major work, La Galatea, in his late thirties, and also wrote a few plays, but remained impoverished. He was in his late fifties when the publication of the first part of his tale of a bumbling errant knight established him as one of the world's pre-eminent writers.

A MAN IS NOT OLD AS LONG AS HE IS SEEKING SOMETHING.

Jean Rostand

Trailblazer Nan

IN OCTOBER 2014 NAN 'DRAG'N FLY' REISINGER, OF CAMP HILL, PENNSYLVANIA, COMPLETED THE 2,182-MILE APPALACHIAN TRAIL – THE FAMOUS HIKE FROM GEORGIA TO MAINE – WHEN SHE WAS 74 YEARS OLD. SHE BECAME THE OLDEST WOMAN TO FINISH IT.

There are two types of hikers: section hikers and thru-hikers. The former complete their journey in sections, sometimes over several years, while the latter do the whole journey in one go. What makes Nan Reisinger even more extraordinary is that she is a thru-hiker. She left Springer Mountain, Georgia, the southern part of the trail, on 30th March and reached Katahdin, Maine, on 4th October.

Her secret was to walk a little bit every day over a six-month period, with only 15 days of complete rest with no hiking at all: 'I had to keep at it. I couldn't take time off. I couldn't ever hike the real long miles like some younger people do. So we had to hike every day and not take breaks.' She lost 25 pounds during the endeavour and wore out three pairs of shoes. An injury along the way nearly ended her challenge: she tripped and hit her knee on a rock and had to spend a week recovering before backtracking to make up lost ground.

When Reisinger isn't hiking, she stays active by cross-country skiing, canoeing, bicycling, gardening and tap dancing.

Most people say that as you get old, you have to give up things.
I think you get old because you give up things.

Theodore Green

Age is like the newest version of a software – it has a bunch of
great new features but you lost all the cool features the original
version had.

Carrie Latet

LIFE WILL BE OVER SOONER THAN WE THINK. IF WE
HAVE BIKES TO RIDE AND PEOPLE TO LOVE, NOW IS

THE TIME.

Elisabeth Kübler-Ross

ONE CONSOLATION OF AGEING IS REALISING THAT WHILE YOU HAVE
BEEN GROWING OLD YOUR FRIENDS HAVEN'T BEEN STANDING
STILL IN THE MATTER EITHER.

Clare Boothe Luce

Memento Mori

Seeing her aged mother-in-law Margaret wearing a new locket, Allison asked what was inside.

'I keep a lock of your husband's hair.'

'But Mike's still alive.'

'I know, but his hair is gone.'

> I KNOW I'M DRINKING MYSELF TO A SLOW DEATH, BUT THEN I'M IN
>
> ## NO HURRY.
>
> *Robert Benchley*

THE DIFFERENCE BETWEEN A DRUNK AND AN ALCOHOLIC IS THAT A DRUNK DOESN'T HAVE TO ATTEND ALL THOSE MEETINGS.

Arthur Lewis

THE SECRET TO A LONG LIFE IS TO STAY BUSY, GET PLENTY OF EXERCISE, AND DON'T DRINK TOO MUCH. THEN AGAIN, DON'T DRINK TOO LITTLE.

Hermann Smith-Johansson, at age 103

It's Technically Fruit

IN FEBRUARY 2016, ANTONIO DOCAMPO GARCÍA DIED AT THE AGE OF 107. HE ATTRIBUTED HIS LONGEVITY TO HIS LOVE OF WINE. HE DRANK AT LEAST FOUR BOTTLES OF RED WINE EVERY DAY, AND NEVER DRANK WATER.

After his death, Antonio's son Miguel Docampo López explained to reporters that his father enjoyed two bottles of wine with his lunch and another two with dinner: 'When we were both at home we could get through 200 litres of wine a month. He could drink a litre and a half all at once.'

Fortunately, Antonio's drinking habits didn't cause him any financial hardship because he owned a vineyard in Ribadavia in north-west Spain and was founder of the wine company Bodegas Docampo. In a typical year, if he produced 60,000 litres he would keep 3,000 litres for himself, and he always maintained that his organic, chemical-free wine was the secret to long life. He also enjoyed the occasional 'medicinal' shot of brandy with breakfast.

Antonio was also known for his sense of humour and regularly joked, after finishing a meal: 'Give me another glass of wine so I can snore when I'm dead.'

Beautifully Ageing

STATUESQUE FRANCES DUNSCOMBE WAS BORN IN STREATHAM, SOUTH LONDON, LEFT SCHOOL AT 15 AND MET HER HUSBAND, RALPH, THE LOVE OF HER LIFE, WHEN SHE WAS SEVENTEEN.

Fast forward more than sixty years, when Frances found herself newly widowed after nursing Ralph through vascular dementia. She felt 'washed up and hopeless' until she found a new lease of life as a professional model.

Frances's daughter, Tineka, a professional model in her 50s, introduced her mother to the Grey Model Agency in London, which specialises in older models. Its motto is 'Representing the beautifully ageing mature model'.

'I thought they were having a joke,' recalls Frances. 'How could you possibly model at my age? But they were quite serious.' She quickly gained international fame by appearing at London Fashion Week, shooting in Prada A/W 15 for a Hunger Magazine editorial and starring in the ITV documentary, Secrets of Growing Old. In 2016 she was 83 and the oldest model on their books.

Apart from her high cheekbones and aristocratic poise, Frances revealed her secrets for staying hale, hearty and photogenic: 'I eat healthily, I stretch every morning, I dance alone in my bedroom – and I drink half a glass of red wine at lunchtime, which makes me feel awfully "la vie en rose".'

> YOU CAN TAKE NO CREDIT FOR BEAUTY AT SIXTEEN.
> BUT IF YOU ARE BEAUTIFUL AT SIXTY, IT WILL BE YOUR
> SOUL'S OWN DOING.
>
> *Marie Stopes*

I've had to tone it down a bit. But I've still got fabulous legs and wear mini-skirts. I'll keep wearing bikinis till I'm 80 … I will grow old gracefully in public – and disgracefully in private.

Jerry Hall

Be careful about reading health books.
You may die of a misprint.

Mark Twain

CUT OFF MY HEAD AND
I AM 13.

Coco Chanel, at age 60

YOU CAN BE GLAMOROUS AT ANY AGE. IT IS NOT THE PREROGATIVE OF THE YOUNG. IN FACT, THE SELF-CONFIDENCE OF EXPERIENCE IS AN ADDED BONUS.

Joan Collins

Ugly Ducklings

A decrepit retired couple, Roger and Brenda, had finally built their dream home, but the builder had a concern about the position of a window next to the walk-in shower.

'I'm afraid your neighbours may get a good view of you in the buff,' he warned.

Brenda exchanged a glance with her husband and then replied, 'Don't worry. They'll only look once.'

MY IDEA OF EXERCISE IS A GOOD BRISK SIT DOWN.

Phyllis Diller

JOGGING IS FOR PEOPLE WHO AREN'T INTELLIGENT ENOUGH TO WATCH TELEVISION.

Victoria Wood

I HAVE A PUNISHING WORKOUT REGIMEN. EVERY DAY I DO THREE MINUTES ON A TREADMILL, THEN I LIE DOWN, DRINK A GLASS OF VODKA AND SMOKE A CIGARETTE.

Anthony Hopkins

Vanity Spurs Me On

DR CHARLES EUGSTER, A RETIRED BRITISH DENTIST WHO LIVES IN ZURICH, IS LIVING PROOF THAT AGE IS JUST A NUMBER, THE TITLE OF THE BOOK HE PUBLISHED IN 2016 WHEN HE WAS 97 YEARS OF AGE.

He is a world-renowned expert on successful ageing and holds many world records in his age category. He started lifting weights when he was 87 and is now believed to be the oldest competitive bodybuilder on the planet, with a physique and level of fitness that puts many fifty-year-olds to shame.

'Yes, I want to change the world,' he admits. 'I see people half my age huffing and puffing and walking around with fat tummies – tummies that are killing them – and I want to shake them. Do they not understand?'

He is refreshingly candid about his initial motivation: 'One of my saving graces is that I am extremely vain. Vanity spurs me on. One day I looked down and saw these horrible varicose veins bulging on my legs and I thought, "Urgh, I am falling apart".'

However, his passion for exercise has its limits. He proselytises for short sustained bursts of activity that build muscle and believes, 'anyone running a marathon over the age of 50 is doing something very dangerous indeed'.

Go Harriette!

HARRIETTE THOMPSON OF CHARLOTTE, NORTH CAROLINA WAS SEVENTY-SIX YEARS OLD WHEN SHE RAN HER FIRST MARATHON.

Sixteen years later, on 31st May, 2015, aged 92 years and 65 days, Harriette ran the San Diego Marathon in 7 hours, 24 minutes and 36 seconds, becoming the oldest woman to complete a marathon. She was cheered over the finishing line by a huge crowd of awed spectators.

She enjoyed the support but was characteristically modest about her incredible achievement: 'I keep thinking, "I don't deserve this [attention]", but if it helps or if it encourages anybody, it makes me feel good.'

Thompson was a classically trained pianist who performed three times at Carnegie Hall, and she played piano pieces in her head to get her through the race. Her many runs have raised more than $100,000 for the Leukemia and Lymphoma Society, a charity close to her heart as she has lost many friends and family members to cancer, including her husband of 67 years, Sydnor Thompson, who died just four months before her 2015 record-breaking run. In 2016 she had to take a break from running to battle her own cancer, but is determined to return to running, and is even planning to tackle another marathon.

'I think if I can do it, anybody can do it, because I wasn't trained to be a runner. But I have also found that it's very invigorating. I feel like a million dollars when I'm finished.'

For all the advances in medicine, there is still no cure
for the common birthday.

John Glenn

Be not afraid of going slowly, be afraid only of standing still.

Chinese proverb

THE TROUBLE WITH RETIREMENT IS THAT YOU NEVER GET A

DAY OFF.

Abe Lemons

WOMEN NEVER HAVE YOUNG MINDS.
THEY ARE BORN 3,000 YEARS OLD.

Shelagh Delaney

My only regret in life is that I did not drink more champagne.

John Maynard Keynes

I complain that the years fly past, but then I look in the mirror and see that very few of them actually got past.

Robert Brault

IF I HAD TO LIVE MY LIFE OVER AGAIN, I'D BE A
PLUMBER.

Albert Einstein

IF I HAD MY LIFE TO LIVE OVER,
I WOULD PICK MORE DAISIES.

Nadine Stair

So Good

IF YOU HAD TO CHOOSE A POSTER BOY FOR NEVER BEING TOO OLD TO RISE ABOVE A STRING OF FAILURES, HARLAND SANDERS WOULD BE TOP OF THE LIST.

Born in 1890, he dropped out of school and left home at the age of 12 to escape his stepfather, and spent the next fifty years in a succession of dead-end jobs and doomed ventures that included army mule-tender, farmhand, motel operator, horse carriage painter, streetcar conductor and train ash pan cleaner. He was fired from several jobs for insubordination and even pursued a brief legal career, which ended after he publicly brawled in court with one of his own clients. In his early twenties he struck lucky by investing in a ferry boat company but he blew the $22,000 share windfall on a failed venture to manufacture acetylene lamps.

By his forties, Harland Sanders was running a small petrol station in North Corbin, Kentucky, where he also served customers fried chicken in a side room that doubled as his sleeping quarters. Over several years he perfected his secret ingredients and pressure frying technique, and franchised the first Kentucky Fried Chicken in 1952. By the time he was 73 the franchise had grown to over 600 restaurants and he sold the company for $2 million.

Colonel Sanders continues to epitomise the brand he founded, and in his later years was never seen in public without his famous frock white coat and string tie. By the time of his death in 1980, there were an estimated 6,000 KFC outlets in 48 countries worldwide.

> IT REQUIRES A GREAT DEAL OF BOLDNESS AND A GREAT DEAL OF CAUTION TO MAKE A GREAT FORTUNE, AND WHEN YOU HAVE GOT IT, IT REQUIRES TEN TIMES MORE WIT TO KEEP IT.
>
> *Ralph Waldo Emerson*

The Leopard Man of Skye

WHEN HE WAS SIXTY-FIVE, ENGLISH-BORN EX-SOLDIER TOM WOOLDRIDGE ENTERED THE GUINNESS BOOK OF WORLD RECORDS AS THE MOST TATTOOED MAN ON EARTH.

He was known as Tom Leppard or the Leopard Man of Skye, having spent two years and £5,500 covering more than 99 per cent of his body with a leopard-like yellow and black pattern, and he even wore bespoke feline fangs custom-made by his dentist. The lithe pensioner spent twenty years living in a small cottage on the Isle of Skye, Scotland, with no heating or electricity, often clothed solely in a small leopard-skin posing pouch.

Interviewed in 2001, Tom explained that after serving in the army for thirty years, he had found it hard to adjust to civilian, life, so 'I decided I wanted to be the biggest of something, the only one of something. It had to be a tattoo … I thought if I get the biggest of something and live in a strange way people might pay me.' He had no real affinity for big cats, but chose the leopard-skin pattern because he thought it would be easy for a tattoo artist to copy: 'It was a necessary evil to supplement my income support, or latterly my pension.'

Self Assembly

The sight of her aged grandfather cleaning his false teeth fascinated a young girl. She sat rapt as he carefully removed them from his mouth, brushed and rinsed and then pressed them back into place. 'Cool, Grandpa!' she said.
'Now take off your arm.'

SEX AT THE AGE OF 84 IS A WONDERFUL EXPERIENCE. ESPECIALLY THE ONE IN THE

WINTER.

Milton Berle

I REGRET HAVING BEEN SO POLITE IN THE PAST.
I'D LIKE TO TRAMPLE ON AT LEAST A DOZEN PEOPLE.

Harold Brodkey

All Ears

An elderly gentleman bought an expensive hearing aid and the doctor declared, 'Your hearing is perfect. Your family must be really pleased that you can hear again.'

The gentleman replied, 'Oh, I haven't told my family yet. I just sit around and listen to the conversations. I've changed my will three times.'

> WHEN YOU GET TO MY AGE YOU EITHER RUN AWAY OR JUMP IN WITH **BOTH FEET.**
>
> *Jan Leeming*

TO WIN BACK MY YOUTH ... THERE IS NOTHING I WOULDN'T DO – EXCEPT TAKE EXERCISE, GET UP EARLY, OR BE A USEFUL MEMBER OF THE COMMUNITY.

Oscar Wilde

AGE IS NOT MEASURED BY YEARS. NATURE DOES NOT EQUALLY DISTRIBUTE ENERGY. SOME PEOPLE ARE BORN OLD AND TIRED WHILE OTHERS ARE GOING STRONG AT SEVENTY.

Dorothy Thompson

For The Thrill

IN APRIL 2010, AT THE AGE OF 96, SOUTH AFRICAN MOHR KEET OFFICIALLY BECAME THE OLDEST BUNGEE JUMPER EVER WHEN HE JUMPED OFF BLOUKRANS BRIDGE, NEAR NATURE VALLEY IN THE WESTERN CAPE.

He was egged on by his daughter and grand-niece, who both followed him in jumping. After the bungee jump, medics tested his blood pressure and declared him to be in perfect health.

The Bloukrans Bridge is the highest bungee bridge in the world, with a drop of 216 metres (708 feet). Bungee jumpers fall 160 metres before the bungee rope pulls them 120 metres upwards for their first rebound.

The intrepid nonagenarian has faced much peril during his long life, including four years spent as a prisoner of war in France after being captured by a German gunboat on his way back from America.

He also enjoys white-water rafting and parachuting. When asked whether he jumped for the enjoyment or for the challenge, he confirmed that he did it 'for the thrill' and 'actually to get rid of fear … I believe that I have to do things. To live life … to face a challenge, to be able to go through it.'

Long Groove

AMERICAN STOCK CAR RACING DRIVER HERSHEL MCGRIFF IS WIDELY RECOGNISED AS ONE OF THE BEST DRIVERS IN NASCAR SERIES HISTORY.

He started racing in 1945 when he was 17 at the dirt Portland Speedway, finishing 13th in his family's sedan. Five years later he won the Pan American Road Race in Mexico in a 1950 Oldsmobile 88, with an average speed of 79.2 mph over 27 hours, 34 minutes and 25 seconds. His prize was more than $17,000 – a small fortune in those days. He raced until 1955 and then quit for ten years to concentrate on running the family timber and mill business back home on the West Coast.

He resumed racing in the late sixties and was a long-time competitor in the NASCAR K&N Pro Series West. He won the series title in 1986 and enjoyed ten consecutive seasons finishing in the top ten. In 1989, at the age of 61, he became the oldest driver to win a NASCAR feature race.

In 2006, McGriff was inducted into the Motorsports Hall of Fame of America, and declared, 'This is fantastic, getting in the Hall of Fame, but, hey, I might not be through yet.' He wasn't. Despite 'retiring' at the age of 74, in 2009, at the age of 81, he finished thirteenth in a national NASCAR race at Portland International Raceway.

> ## A GREAT PLEASURE IN LIFE IS DOING WHAT PEOPLE SAY YOU CANNOT DO.
> ### Walter Bagehot

Apparently more than 80 per cent of open-top sports cars are sold to sad sacks who believe this throbbing mechanical extension makes them look young and virile, not old and desperate.

Amanda Craig

It's sad to grow old, but nice to ripen.

Brigitte Bardot

IN THREE WORDS I CAN SUM UP EVERYTHING I'VE LEARNED ABOUT LIFE:

IT GOES ON.

Robert Frost

I THINK A LOT ABOUT GETTING OLD.
I DON'T WANT TO BE ONE OF THOSE 70-YEAR-OLDS
WHO STILL WANT LOTS OF SEX.

Rupert Everett

The majority of people perform well in a crisis and when the spotlight is on them; it's on the Sunday afternoons of this life, when nobody is looking, that the spirit falters.

Alan Bennett

THE BEST PART ABOUT BEING OVER THE HILL IS THAT
YOU'RE NOT UNDER IT.

I FINALLY FIGURED OUT THE
ONLY REASON TO BE ALIVE IS TO
ENJOY IT.

Rita Mae Brown

IF WE NOTICED WE WERE GETTING OLDER
ON A DAILY BASIS WE WOULD DO NOTHING BUT SQUAT
IN THE DUST AND FRET.

Griff Rhys Jones

Don't Move, Won't Move

YVONNE DOWLEN FROM COLORADO HAD A CAR ACCIDENT WHEN SHE WAS 80 YEARS OLD, SUFFERING MAJOR CONCUSSION. AT THAT POINT, HER DOCTOR ADVISED HER TO HANG UP HER ICE SKATES.

Ten years later she was still skating, competing and being an inspirational teacher. Yvonne had been skating since she was a young teenager and had toured the world with the Ice Capades, so she wasn't going to stop doing the thing that she loved and that kept her mentally and physically fit: 'If I ever get in a bad mood, I look at my peers with their oxygen bags, put on my skates and smile.'

Yvonne's skating was her personal physiotherapy, and helped her to recover from her car crash more effectively than sitting in a chair. She continued to travel, often with her daughter, Sherry, to competitions across the country. Her motto was, 'If you don't move you won't move.'

She inspired many younger skaters to join the sport, or to take it up again after years away. Those who watched her skate often remarked on the joy which she projected, inspiring others, especially seniors, to share her positive view of the future and ageing: 'I never used to like to admit how old I was when I was forty, but now I am delighted to say I have lasted this long and I am still skating.' Yvonne took part in her final ISI competition just six months before her death in May 2016 at the age of 90.

Exceptional Epper

SEVENTY-FIVE-YEAR-OLD JEANNIE EPPER IS WIDELY CONSIDERED TO BE THE GREATEST STUNTWOMAN WHO'S EVER LIVED.

She was Lindsay Wagner's stunt double in The Bionic Woman, Linda Evans' stunt double for Dynasty (including the famous catfight scene), Lynda Carter's stunt double on Wonder Woman and appeared in 18 episodes of Charlie's Angels. She performed stunts in scores of iconic seventies and eighties films, including The Poseidon Adventure, Blazing Saddles, The Towering Inferno, Logan's Run, Close Encounters of the Third Kind, Blade Runner, Poltergeist, Romancing the Stone, RoboCop and Road House. She was still racking up stunt credits well into her sixties and seventies in top Hollywood films, including Minority Report, Catch Me If You Can, 2 Fast 2 Furious, Freaky Friday, State of Play and Kill Bill: Vol. 2.

In 2015, aged 74, she performed stunts in the action comedy Hot Pursuit, starring Reese Witherspoon and Sofía Vergara. During a career spanning more than fifty years, she has appeared in more than a hundred Hollywood films and she helped found The Stuntwomen's Association of Motion Pictures. Her work was recognised by a Lifetime Achievement Award at the Taurus World Stunt Awards in 2007. For her, failure and retirement are not an option. She told Entertainment Weekly, 'As far as I'm concerned, whenever I do a stunt, it's 150 per cent going to work out.'

> I DON'T HAVE TIME TO THINK ABOUT AGE.
> THERE ARE SO MANY OTHER THINGS TO DO.
> *Ursula Andress*

Homebody

A broker was arranging car insurance for an elderly client. She asked him to estimate how many miles he drove in a year. He didn't have a clue.

'Well, do you drive 10,000 miles a year,' she asked, 'or 5,000?'

After a brief pause, he asked, 'What month is this?'

She told him it was September.

'Maybe this will help,' he replied. 'I filled the car with petrol in February.'

I'M NOT REALLY WRINKLED.
I JUST TOOK A NAP ON A CHENILLE

BEDSPREAD.

Phyllis Diller

YOU KNOW YOU'RE GETTING OLD WHEN YOU OPEN THE FRIDGE DOOR AND CAN'T REMEMBER IF YOU'RE PUTTING SOMETHING IN OR TAKING SOMETHING OUT.

Lottie Robson

I KNOW I'M GETTING OLDER BECAUSE THESE DAYS, BEFORE I LEAVE IN THE MORNING, I HAVE TO ASK MYSELF, 'DID I REMEMBER TO PLUCK MY EARS?'

Christopher Moore

My dad's trousers kept creeping up on him.
By the time he was 65, he was just a pair of
pants and a head.

Jeff Altman

ENJOY KEEPING ACTIVE. REMEMBER – IF YOU REST, YOU RUST.

OLD AGE IS LIKE EVERYTHING ELSE. TO
MAKE A SUCCESS OF IT, YOU'VE GOT TO
START YOUNG.

Fred Astaire

I DON'T PLAN TO GROW OLD GRACEFULLY.
I PLAN TO HAVE FACE-LIFTS UNTIL
MY EARS MEET.

Rita Rudner

The Music Within Me

GAY MCINTYRE IS PROBABLY THE BEST JAZZ MUSICIAN YOU'VE NEVER HEARD OF.

Now in his eighties, the Derry jazz legend practises strenuously and plays the alto sax and clarinet with an emotional power and technique that is second to none. But he was in his late seventies before he released his debut album, The Music Within Me, in 2011.

Gay began playing in jazz orchestras during the 1940s when he was a young teenager, and started his own band when he was sixteen. Two years later, his band supported Nat King Cole at Belfast's Grand Opera House. Afterwards he was summoned to meet Cole, who offered him a job on the spot. Gay turned down this life-changing offer because he wasn't prepared to fly between gigs – and with good reason. Six weeks earlier he had planned to go on holiday with two friends, but a mix-up meant that the airline only sent two tickets. He drew the short straw and was left behind, but the plane crashed, killing both men.

Later he joined the band on Ulster Television's most highly rated programme, Teatime With Tommy, hosted by pianist Tommy James, but he remained a gigging musician, playing the clubs year in year out, including a decade in Belfast during The Troubles.

He's had a tough life on the road, but his passion, discipline and commitment are greater than ever: 'You reach a peak and you're doing pretty well in your playing and you then ask yourself: "Can I push any further forward?"'

Do not grow old, no matter how long you live.
Never cease to stand like curious children before the
Great Mystery into which we were born.

Albert Einstein

In a dream you are never eighty.

Anne Sexton

SOMETIMES IT'S FUN TO SIT IN YOUR GARDEN AND TRY TO REMEMBER YOUR DOG'S NAME.

Steve Martin

YOU ONLY LIVE ONCE,
BUT IF YOU DO IT RIGHT,
ONCE IS ENOUGH.

Mae West